# *Little People,* **BIG DREAMS**™
# ERNŐ RUBIK

Written by
Maria Isabel Sánchez Vegara

Illustrated by
Ben Javens

Frances Lincoln
Children's Books

Ernő was a curious little boy from Budapest, Hungary, who loved spending time with himself. While his mom wrote poems and his dad designed planes, he enjoyed stacking blocks, folding paper, and solving puzzles on his own.

At that time, life in Hungary was very strict. School lasted eight long hours, six days a week, and children spent much of their time sitting still and memorizing facts. Ernő mostly drew and remembered only what sparked his curiosity.

Since Ernő loved colors and shapes so much, he decided
to go to art school and learn how to make sculptures.
Yet something didn't feel quite right. He liked making things
that looked good, but he also wanted them to do more.

Instead of becoming an artist, he chose to study architecture and learn how to design buildings. When Ernő finished college, he realized he didn't want to build houses—he wanted to build minds. So, he applied for a job as a teacher.

As soon as he started teaching design and architecture,
Ernő felt lucky to have a job that didn't feel like work.
He loved spending time with his curious students. They built
things, tested ideas, and learned together in the studio.

Ernő wanted to help his students understand how objects
move and change shape, so he started connecting
small pieces of wood together. It took time and patience,
but slowly, a strange and clever object began to appear.

When Ernő took it to school, his students were amazed. It was a cube made of smaller cubes, and each one could twist and turn without falling apart. But once it started moving, it was hard to remember where each piece went.

To easily follow each piece's move, Ernő added colored
stickers to every side. Then he scrambled the cube,
and the colors moved in ways he didn't expect.

It took him a month of twisting and turning
to return each side to a single color.

As soon as Ernő gave the colorful cube to one of his friends,
they couldn't put it down. Some laughed, some groaned,
but no one wanted to give it back. That's when Ernő decided
to take his cube to a small company that made games.

No one could have guessed how far that little cube would go! In just a few years, more than 100 million people were playing with Rubik's Cube. From kids to grown-ups, everyone was hooked by its endless possibilities, but only one solution.

With some of the money he made, Ernő opened the Rubik Studio—a place where inventors and young designers could bring their ideas to life. He also helped students visit new places and learn how design could change the world.

WHAT WILL YOU CREATE TODAY?

As the years passed, the Cube kept amazing new generations. Some solved it in under four seconds. Others did it blindfolded, underwater . . . or with their feet! Ernő even wrote a book, sharing what the puzzle had taught him.

TALENT DAY
CUBED

And by following his curiosity, piece by piece and idea
by idea, little Ernő shared something big with the world:

the joy of solving, creating, and thinking in new ways.

# ERNŐ RUBIK

(Born 1944)

1980

1986

Ernő Rubik was born in Budapest, Hungary, to very creative parents. His mother was a poet and his father was an aircraft engineer. Ernő was a curious boy, and inspired by his father's engineering skills, he loved to make things. His curiosity continued to grow, and in 1958 he went to a special art school to study sculpture. After school, Ernő wanted to learn even more and went on to study architecture in college. He then became a professor, helping students discover their talents. During this time, Ernő used models to teach his students to understand different elements of construction and design. He wanted to make a structure with pieces that moved without falling apart, and spent hours working on it. His first creation was hand-carved from wood. When he shared it with his students,

2014

2024

they loved it! Ernő continued to tweak his invention, and by 1977 his "Magic Cube," as it was first called, was released in Hungary. Three years later, a US toy company brought Ernő's invention to the world, changing the name to "Rubik's Cube." It was a hit! It won awards, sold millions, and became one of the most loved toys ever. Ernő used his success to open the International Rubik Foundation, where young inventors, designers, and engineers could bring their own ideas to life. Later in his career, he also invented other toys and became an author. But above all, he has kept following his curiosity, taking pleasure in the joy of finding new puzzles to solve. And today, Rubik's Cube still entertains and challenges people with its fascinating design.

Text © 2026 Maria Isabel Sánchez Vegara. Illustrations © 2026 Ben Javens
Original idea of the series by Maria Isabel Sánchez Vegara, published by Alba Editorial, S.L.U
"Little People, BIG DREAMS" and "Pequeña & Grande" are trademarks of
Alba Editorial S.L.U. and/or Beautifool Couple S.L.
First published in the US in 2026 by Frances Lincoln Children's Books, an imprint of The Quarto Group.
Quarto Boston North Shore, 100 Cummings Center, Suite 265D, Beverly, MA 01915, USA
Tel: +1 978-282-9590 **www.Quarto.com**
EEA Representation, WTS Tax d.o.o., Žanova ulica 3, 4000 Kranj, Slovenia. www.wts-tax.si
All rights reserved.



ISBN 978-1-80570-286-3
Set in Futura BT.

Published by Juliet Matthews · Designed by Sasha Moxon, Izzy Bowman, and Karissa Santos
Edited by Lucy Menzies · Editorial management by Izzie Hewitt
Production by Robin Boothroyd
Manufactured In Shanghai, China CC012026
1 3 5 7 9 8 6 4 2

Photographic acknowledgments (pages 28-29, from left to right): 1. Studio portrait of Ernő Rubik, surrounded by piles
of his invention, the Rubik's Cube, c. 1980. (Photo by Pictorial Parade/Getty Images.) 2. Ernő Rubik poses with two
of his inventions, the Rubik's Cube and Rubik's Magic. London, England. November 3rd, 1986. (Photo by TPLP/Getty Images.)
3. Brussels, Belgium. March 28th, 2014. Ernő Rubik is posing with a Rubik's Cube after an event for the 40th anniversary
of the creation. (Photo by Thierry Tronnel/Corbis via Getty Images.) 4. Ernő Rubik sits next to several Rubik's Cubes
on April 29th, 2024. (Photo by ATTILA KISBENEDEK/AFP via Getty Images.)

# Collect the *Little People*, **BIG DREAMS**™ series:

Scan the QR code for free activity sheets, teachers' notes and more information about the series at www.littlepeoplebigdreams.com